Clear the Clutter,
Find Happiness

D0013639

Clear the Clutter, *Find Happiness*

One-Minute Tips for Decluttering and
Refreshing Your Home and Your Life

DONNA SMALLIN

Storey Publishing

*The mission of Storey Publishing is to serve our customers by
publishing practical information that encourages
personal independence in harmony with the environment.*

Edited by Deborah Balmuth and Lisa H. Hiley
Art direction and book design by Carolyn Eckert
Text production by Jennifer Jepson Smith

Cover and interior illustrations by © Zoë More O'Ferrall/Illustration Ltd.

Storey books are available for special premium and promotional
uses and for customized editions. For further information, please call
1-800-793-9396.

Storey Publishing, 210 MASS MoCA Way, North Adams, MA 01247,
www.storey.com

Printed in the United States by Dickinson Press
10 9 8 7 6 5 4 3 2 1

Library of Congress Cataloging-in-Publication Data

Smallin, Donna, 1960–
  Clear the clutter, find happiness : one-minute tips for decluttering and
refreshing your home and your life / by Donna Smallin.
    pages cm
  ISBN 978-1-61212-351-6 (pbk. : alk. paper)
  ISBN 978-1-61212-352-3 (ebook) 1. Storage in the home.
  2. Orderliness. 3. House cleaning. 4. Happiness. I. Title.
TX309.S626 2014
648'.5—dc23
                                        2014028770

To Mom, for always making it look easy.

Introduction

To many people, a clean home means an uncluttered home. An uncluttered home certainly looks cleaner. And less clutter makes cleaning a lot easier. Plus, less mess also means less stress and that makes for a happier home.

I'm excited to share with you hundreds of my favorite tips for everyday decluttering, organizing, and cleaning. Many of these tips focus on ways to save time, reduce those piles of clutter, and help you keep your home more organized with less effort. After all, there's more to life than good housekeeping – and the quicker you get your chores done, the quicker you can have fun doing whatever you love doing.

Every tip can be read in a matter of seconds; many can be implemented in as little as one minute. I guarantee that if you adopt even some of the tips in this book, you will soon be enjoying a cleaner, less cluttered home, which will create greater happiness for everyone living there.

— DONNA SMALLIN

Clear the clutter, clear your mind, be happy!

Often, the biggest obstacle to a goal is ourselves. Get your brain in gear and ask, "What could I be doing differently to obtain the results I want?"

If you want a cleaner, happier home, stop wishing you had a magic wand; become the magic wand.

Where to start?

You don't have to stop everything to get organized; you just have to start. Start *somewhere* right now.

Start with the most visible.

Tackle the stuff on the floor and countertops, for example. Then work your way inside cabinets and drawers. Seeing clear and obvious results will boost your confidence.

Start with something small.

Choose a purse or glove compartment or junk drawer. Empty it completely. Sort into four categories: keep, toss, relocate, or donate/sell.

Start with one thing.

Do one thing that will make your life easier. For instance, if you are always searching for your keys, put a hook or basket by the door for them.

When you feel overwhelmed by cleaning or organizing chores, pick a specific task and set a timer for 15 minutes. Work uninterrupted until the timer goes off. Take a short break and then begin again or start another task.

Every time you cross a cleaning or organizing chore off your "to do" list,

reward yourself

by doing something on your "can't wait to do" list!

"If I had 20 minutes to evacuate my home and could take only what fits in my car, what would I take?"

Most things can be easily replaced. Once you realize this, it's easier to lighten your load.

*Look at decluttering
as an opportunity to share
your abundance.*
There are people who could really
use the stuff you aren't using.

Clutter serves no purpose;
it just takes up valuable space
in your home and creates
unnecessary stress and extra work.

Clutter is what
you end up with
when you have
more stuff
than you need.

Break It Down

Breaking big projects into mini-projects to complete over several sessions makes it much easier to accomplish your larger goal. For example, to declutter your closet:

- Move the clothes you love and wear to one end of your closet. Then, working for just 15 minutes at a time or by the yard on your closet rod, place clothing you have not worn in a year or more in a box or bag.

- In your next decluttering session, pick up where you left off. Spend one session focusing on shoes and accessories and another on the piles of stuff on that top shelf or those boxes that have been buried in the back for so long.

- Finally, if you really want an organized closet that makes it easier to find what you want, arrange items by type of clothing (blouses, skirts, slacks) or by color — or by type *and* color if you have a lot.

If I acquire as
much as a stone,
it owns me
because I will
have to dust it.

—*Henry David Thoreau*

Schedule time to play "dress-up."
Try on everything you own. If it fits
and makes you feel fabulous, hang
it back up. It's a keeper. Donate or
sell anything that doesn't make the
cut. Invite a friend to help you make
decisions, then do the same for her.

Sort clothing into piles —
A, B, and C.

- The A pile is for clothes you definitely want to keep.

- The B pile is a "maybe" pile.

- The C pile is the stuff you no longer love or never wear for whatever reason.

Go back through the B pile and put items into either the A or C pile.

Get rid of the C pile.

DO THE MATH

You say you have no time to declutter your home?

Do you have 10 minutes?

10 minutes a day

× 7 days a week

× 52 weeks

3,640 minutes, or 60 hours

You can do a lot in 60 hours!

"Take five"

every night to pick up
and put away items,
fluff pillows,
and generally tidy up.

Be happy
with what you have.
It is more
than enough.

Change your surroundings and you can change your life.

You might find that letting go of clutter is the start of a new you!

Keep or Toss Quiz

Have I used this item in the past year?

O Yes   O No

Will I need it on a definite date in the future?

O Yes   O No

Do I need to keep it for legal or tax purposes?

O Yes   O No

**Would it be difficult to get another
if I needed it again someday?**

O Yes   O No

If you answer no to every question, toss it.

It's very nice of you to keep things that rightly belong to your grown children, but if they really wanted that stuff, they would come and get it. Set a time limit and let them know that you will donate everything after the deadline — and mean it!

GOOD IDEA!

LETTING GO

If you are reluctant to let go of some things, box them up, write the date on the box, and store it out of the way. If you need something, you can find it. If you have not needed to retrieve anything in that box after one year, you obviously can live without it. Donate the box to charity.

If you are finding it difficult to let go of an item from your past, such as an old prom gown or children's artwork, taking a photograph of the item for memory's sake may make it easier to let go.

Don't try to find the perfect recipient for every item.

Donate to a single charity that will accept everything and let them find recipients for you. Goodwill and the Salvation Army are good places to begin.

Post any item you are willing to give away at www.freecycle.org, a community-based recycling resource. If someone wants it, they will contact you via e-mail and you can arrange to put it on the front porch or at the end of the driveway where they can pick it up on a set day.

Reward Yourself!

Decluttering your home is rewarding
in and of itself, but you can
add some incentive. Decide in
advance on a reward for completing
each major decluttering project.

FLOWERS
*Buy yourself
flowers for clearing
off the dining room
or kitchen table.*

MASSAGE
*Treat yourself to
a massage after
cleaning out the
garage or basement.*

MORE BOOKS

Use the money you earn from selling used books to buy yourself some new books — or even an e-reader.

NEW CLOTHES

Take gently used clothing to a consignment store and buy yourself one new outfit.

AN EVENING OUT

Reorganize a closet, then go out and enjoy dinner or a movie with a friend.

Tackling all the housework yourself doesn't do your children any favors.

- Have them help with laundry, dishes, cleaning, and other chores. You'll be teaching them valuable life skills.

- Try the job jar method of assigning chores: Write each task on a slip of paper and put them all into a jar. Every week, family members choose a chore from the jar.

- Don't just yell at your kids to "Clean up your room!" Be specific about what you want them to do, such as, "Put your dirty clothes in the hamper, put toys where they belong, and make your bed."

Did you inherit clutter?

Perhaps you ended up with all of your parents' belongings when they died and you're overwhelmed with too much stuff, as well as guilt about not wanting it. What would your parents want for you? Would they be happy knowing that you are unhappy?

What if you decided to keep the items you love — the ones associated with happy memories — and sell the rest at an estate sale or auction? Then you could donate the proceeds to a favorite charity in their names.

How is clutter affecting the quality of my life? Is it taking a toll on my self-esteem or relationships?

For quick,
noticeable results,
start the clutter-clearing
process by removing the
biggest items first and
then working your way
down to smaller things.

Progress is the path
to your goal.
Sometimes that path is like a
highway that you travel at top speed.
Other times, it's more like a
scenic byway. Go where it leads you.
Rest when you need to.

Stop paper piles!

- Toss all junk mail. Don't sweat it . . . more is on its way!

- Keep only current catalogs you order from and recycle old ones promptly.

- Cancel magazines you never seem to have time to read and request a refund for the unused part of your subscription.

- Jot notes, reminders, and phone numbers in a small spiral notebook or note-taking app instead of relying on bits of paper and sticky notes.

Find info fast.

- A three-ring binder is a good place to store frequently referenced information such as school schedules and activities, take-out menus, and information for the babysitter, house sitter, or dog sitter.

- Use the inside of cabinet doors to hang important phone numbers, school calendars, and sports schedules.

File it and forget it.

- Designate one basket or tray as your inbox. Do not return papers to your inbox once you remove them. Move them along to the appropriate folder or to the recycling bin or wastebasket.

Go paperless.

- Opt for electronic billing statements from your bank, credit card, and utility companies.

- Scan receipts and important documents to your computer using a scanner with software that allows you to search documents for keywords. Then shred the paper.

- Create folders on your computer that mirror your paper folders for receipts, insurance policies, and so on, and file electronic statements and scanned documents in these folders. Be sure to back up regularly to an external hard drive or secure online service for safekeeping.

Time Saver

How much time do you waste every day looking for your car keys or phone, unpaid bills, checkbook, or whatever? Find a home for these things and never, ever put them down except where they belong.

My mantra:
Don't just put it down, put it away.

Assess your situation.

Have you always had so much clutter?

Or was there an event that tipped the scales in the direction of more clutter? If you have led a relatively uncluttered life in the past, then you are capable of doing so again.

What you
do every day
matters more
than what you do
once in a while.

— *Gretchen Rubin,*
The Happiness Project

Get a little help from your friends. Pair up with a friend who also wants a cleaner home. Set weekly goals and hold each other accountable for accomplishing various tasks throughout the week.

Or commit to helping each other with big projects like cleaning the garage and basement. It's more fun than going it alone.

Think your home cleaner.

Imagine how good you are going to feel in a cleaner, less cluttered home.

Remember that feeling whenever you are tempted to dump a pile of mail on the kitchen counter or buy one more thing you don't need.

Picture yourself smiling as you relax in your happier home.

That
which we
resist
persists.

If you feel overwhelmed

by clutter and an endless list of
household chores that never seem
to be finished, consider that your
feelings may arise from resistance.

Think about why you are resisting.
Be willing to "open into" the process
of cleaning. Continuing not to
do anything about the clutter will
only increase your sense of being
overwhelmed.

Clean Out
That Closet

- If you can't bring yourself to let go of clothes you hope to fit into again someday, put them away with your out-of-season clothes. Maybe you'll be ready to part with them next time you see them.

- Separate shoes into regular wear and occasional wear. Keep those you wear regularly visible and accessible. Store the rest in shoe-boxes (to keep them from getting dusty) at the top or back of your closet or under your bed.

- Move special-occasion clothes to one side of your closet or to another closet to make it easier to get to everyday clothes.

- Buy clothes in coordinating shades. You'll need fewer shoes and accessories to go with your outfits, and you'll enjoy having more space in your closet.

- Set a timer for one minute. Quick! Remove five items from your closet to give away or sell.

"What is the one thing I really need to do that I am avoiding?"

Take a big breath and start working.

What are you doing that contributes to the clutter and mess in your life?

Pick your single worst disorganizing habit and work on changing that behavior over the next month. For example, if you often come home with new purchases but can't figure out where to put them, don't buy anything else until you find a home for those items.

Or if your shoes, keys, purse, coat, and other items wind up in a pile by the door when you come home, make it easier to hang or stash all that stuff neatly but still nearby.

Make today
the day
you declare
your
freedom
from clutter.

What's on your organizing to-do list?

Remove one thing that is not really a priority right now.

There. Now you have time to do something else to create a cleaner, happier home.

Now jump in and finish one small organizing project that's been on that list forever.

What Are You Waiting For?

Use the time you spend waiting to do one quick chore.

WHILE THE SHOWER HEATS UP (1 MINUTE)

- Give the sink and faucet a quick wipe.

- Replace dirty towels with clean ones.

Have a headset? Catch up with family and friends on the phone while you clean. Do your least favorite job (like cleaning the bathroom) or spend some time dusting or sweeping while you chat.

Do the hardest job or the one you dislike most first. Then do whole-house chores like dusting and vacuuming, going from one end of the house to the other. Finish with mopping the kitchen floor.

Inspire yourself:

Post a picture or two
on your fridge
or by your desk that
portrays how you
would like your dream
home to look.

ORGANIZE DRAWERS

What better way to spend a rainy day than catching up on some old television programs — and doing some organizing! Just pull a drawer out of its cabinet and bring it into the family room. Empty the drawer and sort the contents while you watch. Toss the junk. Set aside items to donate or sell. Put back the rest. Repeat until the sun comes out!

Our experiences are driven by our beliefs. If you believe that nothing you do will make a difference, that will be your experience.

A clean home doesn't happen by itself. Regular upkeep is the key.

Start each day with a "clean home" habit like making the bed or doing a quick pick-up before leaving for work so you can return to a fresh-feeling home.

Hire a Pro

Consider hiring a professional, even if it's just to help you get started.

ORGANIZING
Check with the National Association of Professional Organizers at www.napo.net to find an organizer who will show you how to get organized and stay organized.

HOUSECLEANING
After you have your household clutter under control, hire a maid service once or twice a month to help keep you on track.

WINDOW WASHING

A professional window washer can do the job faster and better than you can — and you won't have to worry about falling off the ladder!

CARPET CLEANING

Regular cleaning by a professional carpet cleaner will help your carpets last longer, making it well worth the reasonable cost.

Start acting
more organized
and you will become
more organized.

Clutter is
physical proof of
abundance.
Take a look around.
If you have clutter,
you're richer than you think.

Organize a swap party.

Bring things you no longer want or need and exchange them for things you do want or need. It's a fun, free, and eco-friendly way to get "new" clothing, furnishings, books, and more without spending a dime. Donate anything that is left over.

"What do I stand to gain by having a cleaner, happier home?"

The way to get what you want is to take action. Now.

Don't overwhelm yourself

by thinking about all the work you have to do. Focus more on what you have accomplished rather than what remains undone.

Just do what you can do today.

Take it one room at a time! And if that's too much, take it one shelf or one drawer at a time.

Once an item enters your possession,

you are not obligated to hang on to it forever. Give yourself permission to let go and enjoy the sense of liberation that results.

Minimize future mess.

Make a conscious decision to stop adding to existing piles. Then start going through those piles one by one until they are gone.

Time Saver

Align books with the outer edge
of shelves to avoid dust buildup
on those edges and make dusting
a snap.

The next time you hear
yourself complaining
about not having time to
clean up your home, stop.

All we have is time.

How we choose to use
it is up to us.

Instead of blaming yourself for allowing too much stuff to remain in your home, forgive yourself and move on.

GOOD IDEA!

The unused stuff that's just taking up valuable space in your home might be stuff that someone, somewhere, could really use. Go on a scavenger hunt for "treasures" that you don't need. Pack those items up and take them to a donation center.

Even easier, go to Donation Town at www.donationtown.org to find a local charity that will pick it up!

Think of decluttering as a gift you give yourself.

If at first
you don't succeed,
just pick up
where
you left off.

Make cleaning more fun!

- **Buy sponges and cleaning cloths in bright colors and patterns.**

- **Choose cleaning products in scents you love (three of my favorites are citrus, lavender, and clean linen).**

- **Do some cleaning for 15 minutes. Then read an article in your favorite magazine or a chapter of a book (just one!). Repeat until the job is done.**

Make cleaning easier.

Keep cleaning supplies and tools where you use them, such as a toilet brush in every bathroom, paper towels under the kitchen sink and in the laundry room, or a second vacuum cleaner on the second floor. The time you save by quickly accomplishing a cleaning task is worth the minor initial cost of doubling up on some things.

***Simplify your life
with organized systems***
for handling routine tasks
like filing bills to be
paid and reminding yourself
to pay them on time.

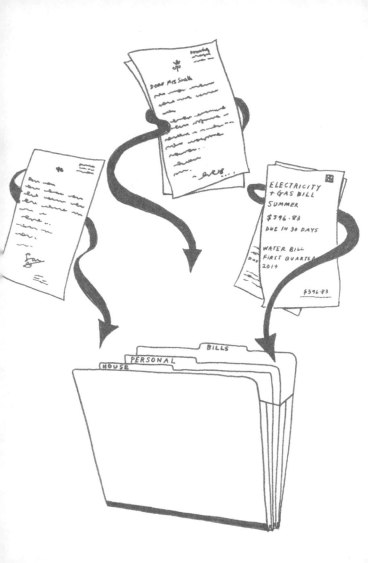

Time Saver

The easiest way to clean your microwave is with steam heat. Place 2 cups of water into a microwave-safe container (add 1 teaspoon of vanilla extract or lemon wedges to the water for a fresh scent). Microwave on high for 5 minutes. The steam will soften cooked-on gunk. Wipe with a paper towel for a quick clean.

To repel fingerprints, smudges, and water marks,

clean your stainless steel appliances with a furniture polish containing orange oil.

Inspire yourself:

Pay attention to
your feelings as you
begin the process
of clearing clutter.
Mindful attention
and acceptance
are empowering.

If you keep putting off a particular chore because you hate it, try timing it. It may not take as long as you think, and once you realize that, it will be easier to make yourself to do it next time. Or trade a chore you dislike with another household member's least favorite chore.

What's in your cleaning caddy?

Stock a caddy with cleaning supplies to tote from room to room, rather than making trips back and forth to your storage closet.
Here is a list of basics for attacking all the everyday cleaning challenges:

- Multipurpose spray cleaner
- Spray bottle of glass cleaner
- Nonabrasive cleaner
- Several microfiber cleaning cloths (or other lint-free cloths)

- Scrubby sponge

- Eraser-type cleaning sponge

- Old toothbrush

- Scrub brush

- Furniture polish and rag

- Special cleaners (stainless steel, leather, etc.)

There's no time
like the present
to get started!

Words are powerful things, especially the words we use when we talk to ourselves. If you catch yourself thinking, "I'm such a slob," immediately negate that thought with "I'm getting better at keeping a clean house."

Establish minimum, non-negotiable standards for your home and family, such as a clean kitchen, organized laundry room, and tidy bedrooms. Whip those areas into shape and then tackle other areas like the bathroom and living room.

Try to enjoy
the process of
clearing clutter.
Disliking it doesn't

make it any easier.

Never leave
a room
without improving

its appearance.

Pick a Day, Any Day

One way to get a cleaner home over time
is to assign specific chores to specific days.
Here's an example:

MONDAY
*Vacuum and dust
living areas.*

TUESDAY
Clean bathrooms.

WEDNESDAY
Clean kitchen.

THURSDAY
Do laundry.

FRIDAY
Clean bedrooms.

SATURDAY
*Tackle a special
cleaning project.*

SUNDAY
Relax!

Avoid comparing yourself to others. Just try to make a little progress each day.

As you pare down your belongings, give thanks for all that has enabled you to have such abundance in your life.

What Are You Waiting For?

Use the time you spend waiting to do one quick chore.

WHILE POPCORN POPS (3 MINUTES)

- Sweep the floor.

- Organize food-storage containers and lids.

- Remove old leftovers and other expired items from your refrigerator.

- Empty or load the dishwasher.

How often do I buy something on impulse only to discover that I really don't like or need it?

If you "shop 'til you drop," clutter is the price you pay. On the other hand, if you think twice before buying things, you may find yourself in a better financial position with less debt and more savings.

Whether you
think you can
or think you can't,
you're right.

—*Henry Ford*

LOADS OF LAUNDRY

If clean laundry tends to pile up before you manage to fold or hang it, here are a few suggestions:

- **When you start a load of wash, take the time to fold and put away any clothes that are in the dryer.**

- **Do a load of towels first because they are easy to fold right out of the dryer.**

- **When you start the dryer cycle, set a timer on your phone or watch and go fold that load right away — before it starts to wrinkle.**

- **Assign a laundry basket to each family member. Have each individual use his or her basket to bring dirty laundry to the laundry room and also to return clean clothes to his or her room.**

If you're overwhelmed by a huge pile of dirty laundry, treat yourself to a "wash and fold" Laundromat service to catch up. Then start building a new habit of doing more frequent loads at home — daily if needed.

The bad news about vacuuming . . .

Experts recommend vacuuming once for each person each week. So for a family of four, vacuum four times a week to prevent dirt from becoming ground in and to extend the life of your carpets.

And the good news . . .

You can get away with vacuuming
just the high-traffic areas regularly,
and vacuuming the rest when
you have the energy and time.
My recommendation: Clean at
least one entire carpet once a week.

Place a decorative bowl or basket on dresser tops or nightstands to collect loose change, pocket items, and everyday jewelry.

Dealing with Paperwork

- **Sort** day-to-day papers into action files: bills to pay, receipts to file, data to enter, papers to photocopy, and papers that require a response.

- **Create** labeled folders for your main categories and store them upright in a stepped desktop organizer or in a filing cabinet drawer in your work area.

- **Free up** space in your filing cabinets. Start in one drawer and work from front to back, eliminating papers and files you no longer need.

- *Use a sticky note* to mark where you left off, so you know where to begin again. Every time you open the drawer, spend a minute doing this.

- *Shred* outdated financial documents and other papers with account numbers to protect against identity theft.

- *Keep* only current insurance policies. When the new documentation arrives, shred the old.

Cut yourself some slack.
Your home doesn't have
to pass the white-glove test.
If you're happy,
that's all that counts.

One of the advantages of being disorderly is that one is constantly making exciting discoveries.

—A. A. Milne

Take advantage of being in a cleaning mood and go at it like a speed demon!

According to a study by the American Cleaning Institute,

eliminating excess clutter would reduce the amount of housework in the average home by 40 percent.

Tackling the Attic, Basement, or Garage

The hardest part of cleaning and organizing a basement, an attic, or a garage is getting started. Schedule a family cleanup day. Or set aside 30 to 60 minutes each week — more if you can — for this project until it's done.

Set up some boxes and sort things into categories such as these:

KEEPERS
Anything you or a family member have used within the past year or that you truly love

DONATIONS
Unspoiled things that someone else might use

SALE ITEMS
Things you can sell at a yard sale or consignment shop or online

TRASH
Anything worn-out or broken and not worth fixing

Hazardous: Watch Out!

In addition to many cleaning supplies, hazardous waste items include:

- Antifreeze
- Brake and transmission fluids
- Car batteries
- Motor oil and gasoline
- Paint and paint thinner

Check with your local household hazardous waste collection program to find out how to properly dispose of these items. Some communities offer an annual collection service.

Every Sunday night,

pick one project
or area to be
the focus of
your cleaning efforts
in the coming week.

When you weigh
the pain of letting go
against the pleasure
of living a happier life,
the choice
becomes clear.

RAINY DAY PROJECT #2

ORGANIZE PHOTOGRAPHS

What you need: A big pile of unsorted photos, some shoe boxes or brown-paper grocery bags cut down to about 6 to 8 inches, and a wide felt-tip marker

Label the boxes or bags to identify 5 to 7 broad categories such as *vacations*, *grandkids*, and *college years*.

Sort the photos into those categories.

When you're done, sort each group into sub-categories. For example, take the vacation photos and sort into new bags labeled *Vacation — (Name of Destination)*.

Organizing is

what you do before

you do something,

so that when you do it,

it's not all mixed up.

— *Christopher Robin (A.A. Milne)*

Plan a Purge

Once a year is good. Twice a year is better. Or do regular mini purges:

JANUARY
Files

APRIL
Household furnishings

MAY
Kitchen and pantry items

JUNE
Bathroom and medicine cabinet

JULY
Sporting equipment

SEPTEMBER
Storage areas

NOVEMBER
Toys

"Is it more important to me to keep this item or to have the space it occupies? What if I were moving? Would it be worth packing and unpacking it?"

That's the stuff that's really important to you. Everything else you could live without if you had to.

***It's surprising how grubby
the laundry area can become.***
Once a month or so, clean the
surfaces of the washing machine and
dryer with my go-to mixture of
1 part white vinegar to 3 parts water.

Don't forget to clean the fabric
softener and bleach dispensers too.
Holding them over a sink, pour a
little of the vinegar/water solution into
them and give them a scrub with
an old toothbrush before rinsing.

Play clutter tag!

To make family members more aware of their clutter trails, start tagging belongings that have been left lying around (those colorful sticky flags designed for paperwork work well). Children may enjoy helping you tag, and you can assign them different colors if you want. Just seeing the tags pile up may make them more aware of putting things away.

Resolve to surround
yourself only
with things you find
useful or beautiful.
Let go of the rest.

What Are You Waiting For?

Use the time you spend waiting to do one quick chore.

WHILE THE BATHTUB FILLS (6 MINUTES)

- Straighten your linen closet.

- Organize your makeup (toss anything you haven't used in the last year).

- Clean the toilet inside and out.

USE IT OR LOSE IT

The hard part of decluttering is
having to make decision after
decision about what to keep and
what to toss. One way to make
it easier is to create umbrella rules
that you can apply to *all* items.
"If you don't love it or use it, lose it"
is an example of an umbrella rule.
"If you have duplicates of something,
keep just one" is another.

Many people find it helpful to add a
time limit. For example, if you haven't
used something in more than a year,
then it's probably time to get rid of it.

In five minutes,
you can pick up and
put away
five things.

Tackle a pile of papers.

Start by flipping over the pile.
Because the papers on the bottom
are older, many are outdated,
making it an easy decision to toss
them. One by one, make a
decision to either file it, act on it
(for example, pay a bill), or toss it.

"Does this belong here?"

Before you set something down,
be it your keys, a pile of mail,
or the broom and dustpan you've
just used, think about finding it
the next time you need it.

Have a backlog of magazines or newspapers to read?

Catch up in one minute by recycling all but the most recent issue or two, and vow to keep up with your reading from here on out. When new issues arrive, recycle the oldest ones.

GOOD IDEA!

PUT "LIKE" WITH "LIKE"

When decluttering, sort items into
two main categories: what to keep and
what to toss. Then sort the keepers
by putting "like" with "like." For
example, put batteries with batteries,
pens with pens, lipsticks with lipsticks.
Use whatever organizing "products"
you have on hand, such as plastic
ziplock bags. Then return the items
to their home.

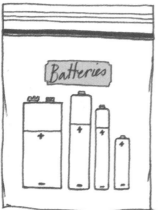

Turn Clutter into Cash

According to an eBay study, the average American has thousands of dollars' worth of unused items that could be sold or donated to a charitable organization for the tax write-off. On the next few pages are some tried-and-true places to sell stuff.

ONLINE

- *Craigslist* This is my personal favorite for large items and anything that you might be selling for $25 or more (little stuff is not worth the drive for most people). Go to www.craigslist.org.

- **eBay** Anything you can ship, you can sell via an eBay auction. Go to www.ebay.com.

- **Facebook** If you have a lot of Facebook friends, create a photo album of things you are selling. Post it and ask your friends if they know anyone who might be interested. You can also search Facebook for online yard sale groups in your city or area.

- **Classified ads** in your local paper may be worth the money if you have large-ticket items, such as a recreational vehicle, snowblower, or tractor.

IN PERSON

- *Estate sales* If you are moving, downsizing, or emptying the inherited home of a loved one, check www.estatesales.net for a company that does estate sales, tag sales, or auctions in your area.

- *Yard sale or garage sale* Once you've set a date, be sure to list your sale on www.craigslist.org and www.garagesalestracker.com.

- **Consignment stores** are good for selling gently used clothing, sporting gear, furniture, musical instruments, and other items. Check your local yellow pages, or find a resale shop by going to www.resaleshopping.com and entering your zip code.

Recognize that you are not the same person you were 10 years ago. Your interests, tastes, and styles have changed. Make a decision to keep only those things that are meaningful to you at this point in your life. That goes for gifts you've received, too.

Remember
that the
most important
things in life...

are not things.

Your time is valuable.

It takes a lot of time and energy to plan and hold a successful garage sale. Consider donating all that stuff instead and taking a tax deduction.

GOOD IDEA!

Avoid washing windows
on a sunny day.
If they dry too quickly,
they are likely to streak.

When paring down your belongings, aim to leave about 20 percent free storage space.

Having less stuff in closets, cabinets, and drawers will make it easier — and less frustrating — to put away and retrieve things in the future.

"What's the worst thing that could possibly happen if I decided to let this go?"

If you can live with the consequences, you can live without the thing.

Keep bathroom countertops clear by storing most items in cabinets and drawers. Stash daily toiletries in baskets, bins, or bags for easy retrieval.

TOSS THOSE TOILETRIES!

Go through the cabinets and drawers in your bathroom and get rid of:

- Makeup more than one year old

- Sunscreen more than two years old

- Perfume more than three years old

- Anything past its expiration date

- Any toiletries you no longer use, even if there's still some left

A layer of dust
is a sure sign
that you should give

away or sell an item.

Don't wait! Once you've made the decision to let go of things, get them out of your home as quickly as possible. Put them in your car to drop off at a nearby donations box or take to a consignment store.

Less Laundry

If your clothes aren't noticeably soiled after one use, hang to air and then wear them again. You'll end up having to do laundry less often. Bonus: Your clothes will last longer!

Fewer Wrinkles

Remove clothes from the dryer as soon as the cycle is complete. Keep a stash of hangers in the laundry room and hang clothes immediately. Designate a place for folding items and keep that area clear!

Don't Fold

Save the time it takes to fold a set
of sheets by putting them right back
on the bed after washing. For variety,
switch to a different set when the
seasons change.

Just Enough

You really don't need more than
two sets of sheets for each bed and
two sets of towels per person —
one in use and one in the wash.
That way, you can't fall too far behind
on laundering linens.

Time Saver

Sock smarts: Give each family member a mesh laundry bag marked with his or her name for dirty socks. Hang it in or near the laundry hamper with the "mouth" open to make it easy to insert items. (Adhesive hooks come in handy for this.) Wash and dry socks in their bags so they stay sorted by owner.

If it takes longer than 60 seconds to decide if you should keep something, you probably don't need it.

Though you can begin to see the result of your organizing efforts immediately,

you can't undo years of disorganization in a few days, weeks, or even months.

So be patient and keep at it. Strive for consistency. As you begin to regain control over your physical space, you'll immediately start to feel better (and happier) about your home and yourself.

Roughly 80 percent of the clutter in most homes is a result of disorganization, not lack of space. Take time to really look at the stuff that never gets put away. Chances are it doesn't get put away because it doesn't have a home. Find a place for everything so you can always put your hands on any item when you need it.

Make Room in Your Medicine Cabinet

Ask your local pharmacy if they collect expired prescriptions. If not, the usual suggestions are:

- Follow disposal instructions on the label. Do not flush medicines down the sink or toilet unless instructed to do so.

- Place the mixture in a sealable bag, empty can, or other container to prevent the drug from leaking or breaking out of a garbage bag.

- Before throwing out a medicine container, scratch out all identifying information on the prescription label to protect your identity.

- Mix leftover medicines with an undesirable substance, such as kitty litter or used coffee grounds. This makes the drug less appealing to children and pets, and unrecognizable to people who go through trash seeking drugs.

Our belongings often end up homeless because we simply have too much stuff.

Clean clothes, for example, might "live" in laundry baskets because drawers and closets are full.

That's when you know that it's time to declutter.

You'll never *find* time to get organized. You need to *make* time.

To decide how to most efficiently store things, use the "Hot, Warm, Cold" rule.

If an item is Hot (used frequently, such as the remote to your television), find a spot where it's handy to where you use it.

If it's Warm (used occasionally, such as a muffin tin), it's okay if you have to cross the room for it or retrieve it from a lower cabinet.

If it's Cold (rarely needed, like last year's tax return or your turkey roasting pan), store it on a high shelf or in the attic or basement.

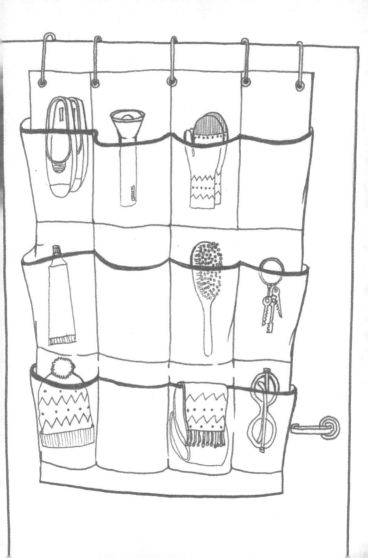

Trying to organize your entire home in a day is like trying to eat a whole cake in one bite. You'd choke! Work on organizing projects in small chunks and strive for consistency.

GOOD IDEA!

Choose five areas where you
most want to be organized.
Your clothes closet?
The kitchen? The mud room?
That basement that's
become the graveyard
for all things unwanted?

Then take immediate action on
just one of them.

*"What does 'organized' look like
to me? How does it make me feel?"*

Then choose a space to organize.
Close your eyes and visualize
what that space will look like
without clutter.

If you can't be a good example, then you'll just have to serve as a horrible warning.

— *Catherine Aird, novelist*

Saving Space

Double-decker turntables provide easier access in corner cabinets and deep cabinets.

Add a hanging shelf under an existing shelf to store cookie sheets, dishes, linens, or other items.

Adjust shelves in cabinets to eliminate wasted space and create more storage.

Use shelf risers in kitchen cabinets to display canned and boxed foods for easy viewing.

Store off-season clothing, shoes, linens, gift wrap, and more in shallow plastic bins or rolling drawers under your bed.

Double your closet space for shorter items by attaching a hanging clothes rod to your existing rod.

Store out-of-season bedding and clothing in vacuum-compressed bags.

Should you
store things
you never use
in the basement,
attic, garage,
or shed?

Careful . . . this is a trick question!
If you don't use those things,
why are you storing them at all?

On your desk and kitchen countertops, keep out only those things you use daily or often. My mantra:

If you use it every day, it gets to stay; otherwise, put it away.

An uncluttered room looks cleaner than a cluttered one. If you pick up more often, you can get away with less cleaning.

Display framed photographs in a grouping on the wall instead of a standing display. This will significantly reduce the amount of dusting you have to do and looks less "cluttery."

Storability
(stor-a-bil-i-ty):

THE ART AND SCIENCE OF STORING ITEMS WHERE THEY BEST BELONG

- Base decisions about what to store, and where, on the level of accessibility required.

- Limit attic storage to things you need only occasionally, such as holiday decorations and tax records.

- Store "like" items (sports equipment, tools, memorabilia) together.

- For easy stacking, buy tubs that are all the same size and label them.

- Use lidded plastic storage tubs rather than cardboard boxes to keep out pests and moisture.

- In the basement, keep storage boxes high and dry on sturdy shelves or pallets.

Today's purchases, especially unplanned ones, become tomorrow's clutter.

"Could I borrow, buy, or otherwise get another one of these if I need it someday?"

In most cases, the answer is yes.

Practice random acts of organizing. If you see something out of place, put it away.
While you're waiting for something or someone, take a few minutes to clean out your purse or a file folder.

FREE ORGANIZING SOLUTIONS

Re-purpose items you are not using as no-cost organizers. Examples:

- Use a muffin tin in a desk drawer to sort paper clips, rubber bands, and other small things.

- Put food-storage containers with no lids in a junk drawer to organize similar items.

- Sort batteries and other collections into ziplock plastic bags.

- Turn a funky old eyeglass case into extra storage in your purse for little items like lipstick.

Periodically sort through your belongings and reevaluate what you really need to keep and what you want in your life. Purchase new items only to replace items that are worn out.

Hang It Up

When looking for more storage space, think vertical.

- Hang shelving, hooks, pegboards, grid systems, or even magnetic strips on walls.

- Hang racks for pots and pans and cooking utensils from the ceiling.

- Hang cup hooks under shelves.

- Hang shoe-bag organizers inside closet doors for things like hats, gloves, sunglasses, and keys.

- Hang a garment bag in a closet for storing vacuum cleaner parts.

With the right systems and shortcuts, you can zip through housework and save hours every month — plus enjoy a cleaner home to boot.

The best system by far is to clean as you go. Doing this can cut your weekly cleaning time by as much as 25 percent or increase the length of time your home can look presentable between cleanings by that same percentage.

The most effective way to teach children to be more organized is to set a good example!

GETTING ORGANIZED

- Don't buy organizing products on impulse. Figure out what you need to organize, then reward yourself with some attractive storage units or a filing cabinet that you'll actually use.

- When it comes to storage boxes, size matters. Smaller storage boxes are easier to move, to stack, and to sort through.

- Label, label, label — stick them on file folders, shelves, storage bins, and boxes.

There will be days when
you might begin
to doubt
if you'll ever be able to
clear your home of clutter.
When you feel like
giving up, remind yourself
why you started.

How to Clean Lampshades

Vacuum lampshades with the dusting brush attachment on your vacuum cleaner. You can also dust with a clean paintbrush, a foam latex sponge, or a lint-removal tool.

How to Make a Bed Easily

For a bed that practically makes itself, replace your top sheet and comforter or bedspread with a duvet and duvet cover. Just whip the duvet back into place and your bed is made.

How to Have a Cleaner Shower

Use a daily "no-wipe" shower cleaner or automatic bathroom cleaner to prevent soap-scum buildup. Squeegee doors and walls after each shower to discourage mildew and minimize water spots.

How to Clean Ceiling Fans

Use an extendable duster that tilts at a 90-degree angle. It's quicker and easier than getting out a ladder — and safer.

Not everything that is
faced can be changed,
but nothing
can be changed
until it is faced.

—*James Baldwin*

"Where would I be most likely
  to look for this?" instead of
"Where should I put this?"

It's a lot easier to keep up than to catch up.

For example, it takes only a few minutes or less to sort through mail every day. The longer you wait, the bigger the pile gets and the more you dread the job. The same goes for doing dishes or laundry.

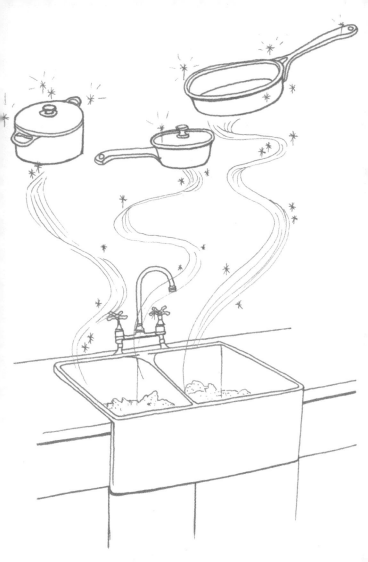

Keep remote controls and other small "cluttery" items in a decorative basket or tin on a shelf just above eye level so all you see is the container. Or use Velcro to attach your TV remote to the TV when not in use.

Down the Drain

Pour boiling water down your bathroom drains once a week to cut through soap scum and hair and prevent backup.

To unclog a slow drain, pour 1 cup of baking soda down the drain followed by 1 cup of vinegar. Let it bubble for a few minutes, then flush with a kettle of boiling water.

Install a continuous cleaning system in your toilet that cleans with every flush. Or brush the bowl every couple of days to keep it clean. Better yet, clean it while you sleep! Pour cleaning product in the toilet before going to bed and just brush and flush in the morning.

Declare one day in the spring and fall as "donation days." Make a note now in your daily planner or calendar and stick to it.

Saving Articles and Information

Here's a good way to save material from magazines and newspapers (for instance, decorating ideas or travel tips or recipes):

- Tear out the relevant articles and store them in a three-ring binder.

- Create a section for each main category, such as "Decorating Ideas," "Recipes," or "Workouts."

- Insert articles in top-loading clear plastic sheet protectors.

- Use tabs to create subsections, such as "Appetizers" or "Desserts."

Creating Extra Storage

IN A CLOSET

Add two or three tension rods all at the same height above an existing shelf to create a new "shelf" for boxes or a small suitcase.

UNDER A BED

Instantly create more storage under a child's bed with a set of bed risers. Use the extra space to store art supplies, toys and games, seasonal clothing, bedding, and more, in labeled plastic storage bins.

ON A COUNTER

Hang paper towels and other necessities under cabinets to get them off your countertop and create more room for food preparation and cooking.

OFF-SITE

Use off-site storage only as a last resort. If you are currently renting storage space, think carefully about the items you are storing. Is it really worth the money to store this stuff? Or could you get rid of some, most, or even all of it?

It's so much quicker and easier to get organized when you have less stuff. So if you aren't using something and don't have an immediate need for it, just let it go. Easier said than done, isn't it?

We tend to develop emotional attachments to our belongings that make it difficult to give them up even when we no longer love them. So we keep holding on to stuff in this unhealthy relationship. Why? Because breaking up is hard to do!

SCARF STORAGE

Clip a set of attractive shower curtain rings together and hang the top ring over a hanger in your closet or a hook on the back of a door; thread scarves through the rings.

CLEAN OUT YOUR CLEANING CLOSET

Evaluate your cleaning tools. Are they in good working order? When's the last time you replaced the vacuum filter? (Yes, you need to do that!) Is your mop head worn out? Make a note of what needs repairing or replacing. If you don't use something, donate it to Goodwill or the Salvation Army, or sell it at your next garage sale.

Next, gather your cleaning supplies. Clear out all those products you don't use or need; give them to a neighbor, friend, or family member. If you haven't used them in the past year, you probably won't ever use them. If trashing, follow the label directions for proper disposal.

Once you've decluttered, organize. Group items by use, such as specialized cleaners for silver and other metals, leather goods, automotive, and so on. Install hooks and wall-mounted holders for mops, brooms, and dustpans. Store clean rags in a hanging bag or a basket on a shelf.

If you don't have a cleaning closet, here's an idea: hang an over-the-door shoe bag with clear plastic pockets behind your garage or laundry-room door to store cleaning supplies.

No time for a thorough spring cleaning?

You don't have to do it all at once. Tackle one room at a time. In a bedroom, for example, you might wash curtains and bedding, clean under and behind furniture, declutter, and organize closets and drawers.

One of my favorite cleaning tools is a lightly dampened microfiber cloth.

Spray the cloth with water and use it to clean smudges from stainless steel appliances, glass surfaces, and mirrors. Just wipe and allow to dry for a lint-free, streak-free clean. The cloth can also be used dry to spot-clean tooth-paste spatters and smudges from glass.

"On a scale of 1 to 10, with 10 being the highest, what is my comfort level with the amount of stuff I have?"

If you answer "5," then reducing your belongings by about half might feel just right.

Stash often-used cleaning supplies, such as cleaning or disinfecting wipes, in places where they are handy for quick cleanups. For example, tuck dusting cloths behind books on a bookcase for dusting on the fly.

Quick Cleanups
for Company

Company coming any minute?
If you don't have a lot of time
to clean, focus on these areas:

BATHROOM

- Give the toilet, sink, and mirror
  a quick wipe-down, and spot-clean
  the floor.

- Put out fresh hand towels
  (or just shake and rehang if they
  aren't dirty or wet).

- Close the shower curtain.

- Empty the wastebaskets.

KITCHEN

- Neaten and wipe kitchen countertops.

- Stash dirty dishes in a dishpan under the sink.

GENERAL

- Go through "public" spaces with a laundry basket to collect any clutter and then stash the basket out of sight with a promise to yourself to put stuff away when your guests leave!

- Close doors to rooms that are off-limits to guests.

Fridge Smarts

- Designate space for leftovers, preferably front and center so you don't forget they are in there.

- Use all same-size leftover containers so you can stack them together. (Square and rectangular containers make better use of space than round containers.)

- Add a large carousel tray or several smaller ones to one or more shelves for easier access to jars.

- Fill a small bin with healthful snacks for you and/or your kids.

- Store unwashed fruits and vegetables in reusable "green bags" to prolong life and keep your crisper bins clean and bacteria-free.

- Line drawers with paper towels to catch drips and spills and replace as needed.

- Clean your refrigerator when it's more empty than full (it's quicker and easier that way!).

- Save future cleaning time by wiping sticky jars and containers before putting them back in the fridge.

Try some green cleaning with these effective cleaning solutions from the pantry:

Distilled white vinegar is my go-to cleaner. Mix 1 part vinegar with 3 parts water in a spray bottle to clean countertops and sinks. Spritz and let sit for about a minute before wiping with a microfiber cloth. Bonus: the vinegar sanitizes as it cleans.

Baking soda is a nonabrasive scrubbing agent. Just sprinkle it on a wet sponge or directly on the surface. For extra cleaning power on greasy surfaces, make a paste of baking soda and water. Apply with a scrubby sponge. Rinse off residue with a clean, damp cloth.

Everything

should be made as

simple as possible,

but not one bit simpler.

— *Albert Einstein*

CLEAN UP YOUR ACT

Having the right tools on hand will help to make quick work of house-cleaning. Get rid of cleaning products and tools you don't use so it's easier to retrieve and put away the ones you do use. Then update your cleaning tools if needed. Examples:

- A vacuum cleaner with a **HEPA** filter captures and keeps allergens out of the air.

- A steam mop is far easier and more effective than a regular mop — and it sanitizes at the same time.

- An extendable duster with micro-fiber head makes quick work of cleaning ceiling fans and other high surfaces.

The average kitchen sponge has as many as 7 billion germs.

After using them, wash sponges and dish cloths in hot, soapy water and rinse. Disinfect daily by zapping them — wet — in the microwave on high for 30 seconds. Or drop the sponges in the dishwasher every night to clean and sanitize them along with your dishes.

CLEAN SPONGES

Have several sponges in rotation:
one in use, dirty ones in the
dishwasher with dirty dishes,
and clean ones at the ready.

Designate a family donations box
for collecting items. Look for one thing
each day that you could donate. Put
it in your donations box. Encourage
family members to do the same. When
the box is full, put it in your car and
take it to a local charity on your way to
or from work.

WHAT TO WEAR

At the beginning of each season, hang clothing with the hanger hook facing out. Throughout the season, as you re-hang items you've worn, hang them normally. At the end of the season, you can easily tell which items you did not wear. Donate them.

The closer a hamper is to where household members get undressed, the more likely it is that dirty clothes will end up in it.

Bathroom Blitz

*Spray your bathtub/shower
with a foaming cleaner that does the
"scrubbing" for you.*

*While that does its work, pour
toilet-bowl cleaner in the toilet.*

*Clean mirrors, countertops, sinks, and
then the toilet lid and outside of bowl.
Go back and rinse the bathtub/shower.*

Brush and flush the toilet.

*Vacuum or sweep the floor and
mop if needed.*

With
less mess
comes
less stress.

Once your home is clean and organized, keep it that way with these three Ps:

- *Preventive* measures significantly reduce the amount of cleaning you need to do.

- *Purging* your belongings regularly keeps clutter to a minimum.

- *Practicing* new habits lets you zip through household chores like a pro.

Clean smarter, not harder.

- Clean from top to bottom. Start with the cobwebs near the ceiling. Then dust the ceiling fans, tops of bookcases, and other higher-up surfaces. Clean the floors last.

- Instead of removing everything from surfaces, move everything to the right to clean the left side, and vice versa.

- After spraying a cleaning product, give it a few minutes to do its job.

- Clean floors in each room in a clockwise direction, starting from the door and finishing up in the middle.

- When washing windows, wipe back and forth on one side of the glass and up and down on the other. If there's a streak, you'll know which side it's on.

- Clean your microwave immediately after using it. Thanks to the residual steam, you can just wipe it out with a paper towel or damp sponge.

- Find the most efficient routine for you and follow it every time so you can speed through it. Example: Clean the front of the microwave, then the stove top, then the front of the oven, and then the front of the refrigerator, finishing with the handle.

- Let dishes air-dry and save your energy for something more fun!

- Wipe up spills immediately — cleaning a sticky, dried mess takes more time later.

- Stash extra trash bags at the bottom of each can for quick changes.

Every time you see
something that would
take just a few minutes
to do and you think,
"I'll get to it later,"
do it now instead.
Your future
self will thank
you for it.

Time Saver

With a quick daily sweep and spot-cleaning of small spills, your kitchen floor won't need mopping as frequently.

Many of us
tend to hold
on to things

long after their usefulness has expired.
One reason is because of the "poverty
mind-set." We subconsciously believe
that if we let go of something, we won't
be able to replace it.

When you cling to things you don't
need or want anymore, you are holding on to negative energy. You are
also acting, whether you realize it or
not, from a belief that you don't have
enough. Donating those items to others
sends positive energy into the world.

Just get rid of it.

You know you want to!

Have the entire family participate in a household purge twice a year. Ask kids for donations of toys, books, and clothes they no longer use or want. Help them feel good about sharing with kids who don't have any.

Or plan a yard sale and let your kids keep the money they make.

Make It a Habit!

Link chores with key daily activities to remind you to do them. Examples:

Brush teeth	Rinse out the sink and wipe off the faucets
Stop for gas	Empty the trash bag in your car
Get dressed	Make the bed
Get undressed	Put clothes away or in the hamper
Finish eating dinner	Wash the dishes right away instead of leaving them until later
Feed the dog	Sweep the kitchen floor

"Do I still love or value this item?"

If not, it's time to let it go.
Give that thing an opportunity
to be loved by someone else.
Give someone else a chance to
love it. And give yourself the
gift of giving.

A Working Workout

What if cleaning house could help you get in shape and maybe even lose a few pounds? Would that motivate you to pick up a broom more often?

Fact: Doing household chores can burn as many calories as some workouts!

At 180 calories per hour, an hour of vacuuming burns as many calories as 15 minutes of kickboxing. Even just walking around putting things away burns 136 calories per hour.

Plus, the more effort you put into doing multiple tasks, the more calories you burn:

- Light effort = 102 calories/hour

- Moderate effort = 170 calories/hour

- Vigorous effort = 204 calories/hour

Put on some music to liven up your working workout and start sweeping!

Act as if you already have everything you need and your life will be filled with abundance in more ways than you ever imagined.

GOOD IDEA!

PANTRY POINTS

- Place the lids to missing food storage containers under oil and sauce bottles in your pantry to catch drips.

- Store dry goods in clear plastic or glass modular containers (mason jars are a good choice, too) in your pantry to prevent accidental spills and keep items fresher, longer. Bonus: You can more easily see when you are running low on those items.

If you hate folding underwear and socks, don't do it!

Just toss them into a bin or drawer or organize by color in a clear plastic hanging shoe organizer in your closet. It may take a few moments to find a matching pair of socks, but think of the time you'll save folding. It might be just the thing to help keep clean laundry from piling up.

Treat unwanted gifts like flowers. Yes, they express a sentiment you appreciate. No, that doesn't mean you have to keep them forever.

— *Don Aslett*

Keep a small trash bag up front
in your car, plus one or more
behind the front seat(s) for passengers
to use. Empty them out whenever
you stop for gas. (A friend of mine
swears by having a trash bag in front
of each kid!)

Have cleaning tools and appliances ready to go.

For example, empty the vacuum canister or bag when you finish cleaning so you don't have to do it before you start next time.

Consider the
postage stamp:
its usefulness consists
in the ability to stick
to one thing till it gets
there.

—*Josh Billings*

Time Saver

Keep a stain-removal pen in your purse or glove box to treat food and drink stains as they occur rather than struggling with them later.

ORGANIZE YOUR PANTRY

- Remove all foodstuffs from pantry and food storage cabinets and drawers.

- Group like items with other like items, such as canned fruits, cereals, snack foods, grains, etc.

- Look at expiration dates on opened and unopened packages and toss them if they're out of date.

- Collect items that are not likely to get used and donate them to a local food bank.

- Wipe shelves clean.

- Keeping like with like, put items back on shelves with labels facing out. (Stack cans to maximize vertical storage space.)

- If you have a label maker, label the shelves by category so that it's easier to find what you need, and other family members know where to return items.

Maximize your organizing goals by tying them into a larger life goal. Think about how being organized will help you create the time and space you need to pursue a dream or simply enjoy a more peaceful life.

Keep Dirt Outside

- Place doormats on either side of entry doors.

- Institute a "no shoes" rule for your house.

- Keep a boot tray near the door for wet or dirty footwear.

- Sweep or dust-mop hard floors often to prevent dirt from becoming ground in by shoes and chair legs.

If you never set
a larger item
on top of a
smaller item,
you'll spend less time
looking for things.

Make It a Habit!

5-MINUTE MORNING TIDY

- Make bed

- Wipe bathroom countertop and rinse sink

- Rehang towels

10-MINUTE EVENING TIDY

- Sweep kitchen floor

- Pick up clutter

TACKLING PILES

Set up two boxes for organizing stacks of neglected paperwork: one for important papers you need to keep and one for papers you think you should keep. Working quickly, file papers in one box or the other, or in a recycle/shred pile.

The next step is to find a home for the important papers by filing them correctly. Then schedule time to go through the second box and decide if you really need to keep everything in it. Meanwhile, you know where all your unfiled papers are.

Keep credit card and debit card receipts

until you verify amounts on your
monthly statement or by reviewing
your account online. Receipts
for consumables like groceries and
dining out can be tossed. Set up
a "Home Inventory" folder to store
receipts for product purchases
and purge it annually to remove
receipts for items you no longer own.

Time Saver

Line the bottom of your oven (and toaster oven) with foil or a silicone oven liner that can be removed for easy cleaning.

Line stove burner pans with foil to catch spills; replace the foil when it gets dirty.

To prevent mildew and bacteria from developing, always allow countertops and floors to dry completely before setting the cutting board or area rugs back on them.

When you wash a cutting board, let it air-dry on edge rather than lying flat.

Cut the Clutter!

Establishing just one or two of these rules will help you keep clutter from accumulating.

ONE IN/ONE OUT

- For every one item you bring in the front door, send one packing out the back door.

THE "PUT AWAY" BASKET

- Set up a basket in a convenient location. Throughout the day, toss in things that need to be put away. At the end of the day, return those items to where they belong.

CLUTTER-FREE ZONE

- Declare one room off-limits to clutter. Establish rules: If you bring it in, take it out. If you use it in here, put it away before leaving.

THANKS, BUT NO THANKS

- Say "no thanks" to things you don't really want or need. For every item you don't bring home today, you save yourself the headache of deciding what to do with it later.

READ OR RECYCLE

- Put all newspapers into the recycling bin at the end of each day, whether they've been read or not. By tomorrow, it will be old news.

Set a timer for 10 minutes in the morning or evening and clean, clean, clean. Focus on high-traffic areas like the bathroom or kitchen and on tasks that are easily put off, like folding and putting away laundry. Make your kids help out before they watch TV or go off to play.

What's that in your junk drawer?

You can sell that old cell phone!
Check out www.sellcell.com to find
the best offer for your old cell phone.
Or ask at the nearest phone store
about recycling programs that help
those who need phones.

Removable adhesive hooks for easy organizing can go virtually anywhere; you can move them any time without marring surfaces.

Install a couple in your closet or behind a door for airing clothes you will wear again before laundering (instead of tossing them over a chair or on the floor).

Keep the floor of your clothes closet clear for quicker, easier vacuuming.

Store shoes on shoe racks, keep them in an over-the-door shoe organizer, or just toss them all in a basket.

If something breaks
and you replace it,
toss the
broken item.
It is officially garbage.

Imagine trying to find a book in a bookstore without a filing system! That's kind of what it's like when you just put stuff anywhere and everywhere without thinking about where it belongs. Start looking at your home as being made up of zones (rooms) and zones within zones (closets, cabinets, drawers).

Most people wear 20 percent of their clothes 80 percent of the time. If you haven't worn something in the last year, it's probably because you don't like the way you look or feel in it. Are you really likely to wear it in the next year?

CLEAR OUT CLOTHING

Keep a small laundry basket or tote bag in your closet into which you can toss articles of clothing you decide you no longer wish to keep.

A Family Affair

To encourage your kids to put away their stuff, make it easy, and as much as possible, make it fun. For example:

- Let them just throw their shoes in a basket by the front door or in their bedroom.

- Install hooks in strategic locations (closets, bedrooms, bathrooms, entryways) so they can easily hang up their coats, backpacks, and clothes they will wear again.

- Lower closet rods so they can hang up clothing more easily.

Make housecleaning
more enjoyable
by putting on your
favorite music
or listening to
an audiobook while
you work.

A large part of getting organized is learning to act from a place of self-esteem, knowing what we want and don't want to do, knowing what we can and can't do, and taking good care of ourselves.

— *Marilyn Paul*

Don't leave bills, papers, library
books, items that need fixing,
and so on lying around as reminders.
Better: Make a note of what you
need to do and schedule a time to
do it.

Place wastebaskets
wherever trash tends
to accumulate.
Empty them regularly.

Keep on Top of Paperwork

If you "pre-organize" your paper piles, it's easier to deal with them when you have the time to go over them.

- Set up an inbox for mail.

- Designate a basket or paper tray where children can put all school papers that require your attention: permission slips, graded homework and tests, and notices.

- If you pay bills in the kitchen or your kids do homework there, assign specific drawers or set up standing files for each family member to store current papers.

Success is the sum of small efforts, repeated day in and day out.

— *Robert J. Collier*

DECLUTTERING TIP

Always declutter before cleaning. Grab a laundry basket and pick up stray items to put away when you're done cleaning. It's quicker and easier to clean when you don't have to work around piles of stuff.

Bring other family members on board

with your goal of a cleaner, happier home.

Plan a family night out after a big decluttering project. Or agree to put yard sale earnings toward a family vacation or a coveted item like a plasma-screen television.

Clean out your wallet or purse weekly

or even daily to remove receipts and other items that can be filed or tossed.

What Are You Waiting For?

Use the time you spend waiting to do one quick chore.

WHILE ON TELEPHONE HOLD (5–10 MINUTES)

- Open the day's mail; toss the outer envelopes and inserts in bill statements along with junk mail.

- Go through file folders looking for papers you can toss.

Clearing clutter doesn't mean throwing everything out. It's all about figuring out what's really important to you and letting go of what isn't.

Declutter to the power of 10.

Choose to complete 10 small decluttering tasks a day every day without fail. Before you know it, chaos will give way to organization and you'll have the confidence to tackle larger decluttering projects.

Allow it to be easier

than you think,

faster than you expect,

and more fun

than you can imagine.

— *Michael Neill*

Create a happy place where you can feel at peace. It might be a room that is off-limits to other family members, or it might just be a favorite chair or your bed. Make an extra effort to keep that space clutter-free.

Give yourself a "happy uncluttered home" deadline. Schedule a celebration one, two, or three months from now. Offer to host a family dinner over the holidays, plan a party at your house, or commit to participating in an upcoming neighborhood garage sale. Then start chipping away!

Whenever it seems like you need more storage space, schedule a decluttering session.

Inspire yourself:

Set realistic goals.
It's okay if they're simple.
For example, "I don't
have to clean out
that entire closet
tonight. I'll just clean out
that one junk drawer."

Instead of aiming
for perfection, aim
for speed.

Most people
have no idea of the
giant capacity we can
immediately command
when we focus all of our
resources on mastering a
single area of our lives.

— *Tony Robbins*

When it comes to stuff, less is more — more space, more time, more happiness.

Time Saver

Don't file papers that you don't need to save, such as utility bills. Save only the most recent one and toss it when the next one comes in. Better yet, opt for paperless billing statements and eliminate filing altogether.

"Do I need to keep this document for tax or legal purposes?"

If not, shred documents with your Social Security number, credit card and bank account numbers, and other personal information to reduce the risk of identity theft.

GOOD IDEA!

The IRS accepts digital receipts
as valid tax documentation.

Use your smart phone to
snap photos of paper receipts and
then store them on a secure
cloud server like Shoeboxed.com
or Evernote.

The difference between try and triumph is just a little "oomph"!

— *Marvin Phillips*

Reduce the amount of unsolicited mail you receive.

Go to www.dmachoice.org and ask to have your name and address removed from their mailing lists.

Use the first day of fall and spring (or the days you set the clock forward and back) to remind you to do semi-annual chores, such as moving and vacuuming underneath furniture, or purging your wardrobe.

Remember that

all you really

MUST do today is

b-r-e-a-t-h-e.

Chores
do not need
to be done
perfectly.

"Done" is
perfect.

Time Saver

Dust large items like tables, hutches, and dressers with a cloth in each hand to make the job go quicker.

Who do you know whose home always looks the way you want your home to look? Next time you are about to toss something on your kitchen counter or table, ask yourself: "What would [name] do?"

You can choose
to create the life
you want or you can
continue to deal with the
life you don't want.

If you are struggling, join a support group.

On Facebook, search for "Unclutter.com Organizing Support Group," a private group where you can ask questions and get answers and be inspired to declutter, organize, and simplify your life.

What Are You Waiting For?

Use the time you spend waiting to do one quick chore.

WHILE RICE COOKS (20 MINUTES)

- Plan meals for the week and write a grocery shopping list.

- Organize your junk drawer (or other drawers).

- Organize a couple of pantry shelves or a cabinet or two.

When you redecorate,

don't allow the old stuff to take up valuable space in your home. Donate it now and let someone else share in the joy of redecorating.

Do as much as you can, whenever you can. Keep at it.

Only what gets scheduled gets done.

Block out time on your calendar to clear clutter.

Then show up for your appointment.

Clutter be gone!

You set things down with good intentions to pick them up and put them away later. Or you don't know where to file or store something and put off making that decision. The next thing you know, a little mess has grown into a bigger mess and it keeps growing until

1. you commit to change
and
2. you take action.

Fortunately, you don't have to stop everything to get organized. You just need to start.

Seek happiness:

Pick a single tip from this book and do it right now!